IT'S A FACT! Real-Life Reads

MONSTER FISH

by Ruth Owen

Consultant:

Suzy Gazlay, MA
Recipient, Presidential Award for Excellence in Science Teaching

Ruby Tuesday Books

Published in 2015 by Ruby Tuesday Books Ltd.

Editor: Mark J. Sachner
Designer: Emma Randall
Production: John Lingham

Photo Credits:
Alamy: 4–5, 19 (bottom); Corbis: 12–13; Fishing Adventures Thailand
(Jean-Francois Helias): 14–15, 19; FLPA: 4, 24–25, 28–29; Shutterstock:
4–5, 18, 26, 27 (top); Superstock: Cover, 20–21, 22–23; Tourette Fishing: 5,
6–7, 8–9, 10–11, 31; Zeb Hogan: 17; Zina Deretsky: 27 (bottom).

Library of Congress Control Number: 2013920131

ISBN 978-1-909673-62-5

Printed and published in the United States of America

For further information including rights and permissions requests, please
contact our Customer Service Department at 877-337-8577.

CONTENTS

Monster Fish

There are more than 25,000 different types of fish on Earth. Some types live in the ocean. Others live in **freshwater** in rivers or lakes. Some fish feed on plants, while others are meat-eating **predators**.

So how does a fish get to be called a *Monster Fish*? Is it because it attacks crocodiles? Maybe it's because it weighs as much as four men.

Could it be because it is armed with a deadly weapon? Perhaps it's because it looks so freaky, it might give you nightmares!

Whatever the reason, every incredible fish in this book deserves the title of...

Monster Fish!

Monster of the Congo River

In the Congo River in Africa, there lives a terrifying hunter.

Its huge jaws can crunch through bones with ease. Its dagger-like teeth will cut through flesh like sharp knives. Its bite is as deadly as that of a great white shark.

This monster hunts for **prey** in the churning, fast-flowing river. It is one of the most ferocious freshwater predators in the world. It has even attacked humans.

It is the Goliath tigerfish.

Goliath Tigerfish

Goliath tigerfish are the largest members of the tigerfish family. All tigerfish are powerful hunters.

These fish have excellent eyesight. They also have an **organ** in their heads that can detect **vibrations** in water. The vibrations tell a tigerfish that a meal may be moving nearby in the murky water.

Tigerfish can swim at up to 30 miles an hour (48 km/h). Their strength and speed help them hunt in rough, fast-flowing water. They are able to capture less-powerful fish that are struggling to swim. Goliath tigerfish are so strong and fast that they can even attack crocodiles!

Goliath Tigerfish Facts

Length: up to 6 feet (1.8 m)

Weight: can be more than 150 pounds (68 kg)

AFRICA

Congo River

Africa's Congo River is home to the Goliath tigerfish.

Catching a Monster Fish

Many people like to catch giant, powerful fish for sport.

Anglers come to the Congo River from around the world. They hope they will be able to catch a ferocious Goliath tigerfish.

Angler

Most anglers don't kill the Goliath tigerfish they catch, though. That's because it takes many years for a Goliath tigerfish to become an adult and start **breeding**. This means the number of Goliath tigerfish in the river rises slowly.

The Congo River needs these top predators. They keep the numbers of other fish under control. Most anglers who catch a Goliath tigerfish release the fish back into the river alive.

Goliath tigerfish

Mekong Giant Catfish

Some monster fish are mysterious creatures. Very little is known about them.

The Mekong giant catfish lives in the Mekong River in Southeast Asia. It has no teeth, and feeds on plants and **algae**.

Where Mekong giant catfish live

ASIA

Mekong River

China

India

Thailand

N
W   E
S

One fact that is known about this fish is that it can grow to be truly enormous. Scientists think it is one of the largest freshwater fish in the world.

In 2005, fishermen in Thailand caught a record-breaking female fish. She was 9 feet (2.7 m) long. She weighed 646 pounds (293 kg). Scientists hoped the giant fish could be released back into the river. Unfortunately, the fish did not survive.

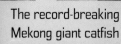

The record-breaking Mekong giant catfish

A Giant in Danger

The Mekong giant catfish is critically **endangered**. It could soon become **extinct**!

This truly mammoth catfish is in danger because of over-fishing. Too many of this fish have been caught by people for food. Also, people have built **dams** on the river. Dams stop the fish from swimming to the places where they breed.

Organizations that help endangered animals are studying this mysterious fish. They want to understand more about how it lives. Then they can find ways to help it survive.

No one knows for sure how many Mekong giant catfish there are. Some scientists think there may only be a few hundred left!

Anglers can help scientists. They catch Mekong giant catfish for scientists to study. Then the fish are released back into the river.

Mekong giant catfish

Giant Freshwater Stingray

The Mekong River is home to another monster-sized fish. This huge creature is the giant freshwater stingray.

No one knows for sure how big these fish might grow. People who live on the Mekong River tell stories about giant stingrays. They say that anglers have hooked these animals on fishing lines. Then the giant fish have pulled the anglers' boats along the river for miles!

Where giant stingrays live

ASIA

Mekong River

China

Pacific Ocean

Papua New Guinea

Thailand

Indian Ocean

Borneo

Australia

N
W E
S

There are many different types of stingrays. Most types live in the ocean. Giant freshwater stingrays live in the Mekong River. They also live in rivers in the areas that are colored red.

Zeb Hogan is a scientist who studies giant fish. In 2008, anglers in Thailand caught an enormous female stingray. Zeb measured the length of its body and tail. The giant fish was 14 feet (4.3 m) long! Zeb studied the fish and then released her back into the river.

Zeb Hogan with the giant freshwater stingray that was caught in Thailand.

A Deadly Stinger

Stingrays are gentle animals. If a predator attacks them, however, they fight back.

Stingrays get their name because they are armed with a deadly stinger. The hard, razor-sharp stinger grows from the fish's tail. A giant stingray's stinger can grow to 15 inches (38 cm) long.

A stingray strikes at an enemy with its whip-like tail. As it strikes, it stabs the stinger deep into its enemy's flesh. The stinger can even pierce through bone. Once the stinger is deep in another animal's flesh, **venom** flows from the stinger. The stingray's attacker is not only badly wounded, it is also poisoned.

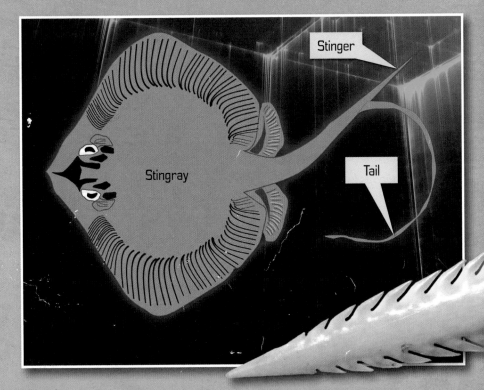

Stinger

Tail

Stingray

Anglers holding a giant freshwater stingray

Stinger

A stingray's stinger has sharp, tooth-like points, like the edges of a saw.

19

Some fish are not monster-sized. They look like something from a terrifying monster movie, though!

Anglerfish live in oceans all over the world. Some types are just a few inches long. Others are up to 3 feet (1 m) long.

An anglerfish hunts using a long body part called a lure. On the end of the lure is a fleshy part called an esca. The esca moves and wriggles in the water. Other fish see this movement. They think it might be food, such as a shrimp. They swim closer to investigate. Then...

CHOMP!

There's no shrimp. Just a hungry anglerfish with a mouthful of deadly teeth.

The fish in this photo look blue because of the lights that were used to take the photo underwater.

Esca

Anglerfish

Lure

Prey

Danger in the Dark

Some deep-sea anglerfish live a mile under the ocean. They live in total darkness at all times.

These hungry anglers have a special way to attract prey. Their lures light up and glow in the dark water. The light is created by a type of **bacteria**. The bacteria live inside the fish's lure.

The anglerfish's prey see the light. They swim closer to investigate. You know the rest!

An anglerfish can open its huge jaws very wide. Its stomach and body can stretch, too. This means the fish can swallow another animal that's bigger than itself.

To catch other fish, an anglerfish uses its lure and esca like an angler's fishing rod and wriggling worm. That's how the fish gets its name.

Glowing lure

Boy Meets Girl

Only female anglerfish have a lure.
That's because male anglerfish
don't need to hunt.

As soon as a male anglerfish is fully grown,
he finds a female. The tiny male bites into the
female's body and holds on. The male then
releases a substance from his mouth.
This substance dissolves the
male's mouth.
It also dissolves
the female's
skin. The two
fish become
joined together.

Female
anglerfish

Next, the male fish starts to shrivel up. Soon, all that's left of him are the body parts needed for breeding. Now the female anglerfish doesn't have to find a mate. Her body has the male and female parts needed for her to produce eggs!

Male anglerfish

Giant Moray Eel

Inside a small, dark cave between some rocks, there lurks a monster. It looks like a huge snake. It has powerful jaws and sharp teeth.

This monster fish is the giant moray eel. It can grow to nearly 10 feet (3 m) long. Giant moray eels live in warm oceans in many parts of the world.

A giant moray eel hunts at night. It waits in its cave until another fish swims by. Then it attacks. The eel's teeth hook into its victim so the animal cannot escape. Then something gruesome happens. A second set of jaws spring forward from inside the eel's throat. These jaws drag the eel's meal down into its stomach!

Giant moray eel

Giant moray eels have long, snake-like bodies.

Jaws of a Monster

Jaw

Second set of jaws

Second set of jaws move forward

Monster Munch!

Many scuba divers want to see a giant moray eel up close.

Sometimes divers carry food to attract the eels. Scuba diver Matt Butcher was feeding sausages to a giant moray eel. Suddenly, the hungry eel bit off Matt's thumb by mistake and swallowed it. Thankfully, Matt survived the accident.

Giant moray eel

Other divers have lost fingers. They put their hands into cracks in rocks. Their fingers were bitten off by eels that were guarding their homes.

Giant moray eels don't attack people deliberately. They are only defending themselves or trying to get food. When divers go into the water, they are in the giant eel's world. A good safety tip is to always watch from a distance. And don't mess with monster fish!

Glossary

algae (AL-gee)
Living things that often look like plants.
Seaweed is a type of algae.

angler (ANE-glur)
A person who catches fish. Anglers usually fish
for sport or as a hobby. They often release the
fish they catch back into the water.

bacteria (bac-TIHR-ee-uh)
Tiny living things that are too small to see with
a person's eyes alone. Germs that cause illnesses
are a type of bacteria.

breeding (BREED-ing)
Mating and producing young.

dam (DAM)
A structure that is built across a river and can be
used to stop the water from flowing.

endangered (en-DAYN-jurd)
In danger of no longer existing. Animals that
are critically endangered are very close to
becoming extinct.

extinct (ek-STINGKT)
No longer existing.

freshwater (FRESH-wa-tur)
Water that does not contain salt.

organ (OR-guhn)
A part of the body, such as the heart or brain, that has a particular important job to do.

predator (PRED-uh-tur)
An animal that hunts and eats other animals.

prey (PRAY)
An animal that is hunted by other animals for food.

venom (VEN-uhm)
A poisonous substance passed by one animal into another through a bite or sting.

vibrations (vy-BRAY-shuhnz)
Small, shaking movements that make something move back and forth, or side to side, quickly.

Index

Read More

Goldish, Meish. *Disgusting Hagfish (Gross-Out Defenses)*. New York: Bearport Publishing (2009).

Owen, Ruth. *Stingrays (Real Life Sea Monsters)*. New York: Rosen Publishing (2014).

Learn More Online

To learn more about monster fish, go to
www.rubytuesdaybooks.com/monsterfish